WORKBOO
STARTE

Series Edit
JoAnn (Jodi) C
Joan Kang Shin

Author
Diane Pinkley

T0045426

Unit 0 2
Unit 1 My School 5
Unit 2 My Toys 9
Unit 3 My Family 13
Unit 4 My Body 17
Units 1–4 Review 21
Unit 5 Stories 23
Unit 6 I Like Food 27
Unit 7 Clothes 31
Unit 8 Animals 35
Units 5–8 Review 39
Writing 41
Cutouts 57

NATIONAL GEOGRAPHIC LEARNING | CENGAGE Learning®

Australia • Brazil • Japan • Korea • Mexico • Singapore • Spain • United Kingdom • United States

Unit 0

1 **Listen.** Look and circle. TR: 2

1.

2.

3.

2 **Listen and circle.** TR: 3

1.

yes no

2.

yes no

3.

yes no

3 **Listen.** Color and say. TR: 4

1.

2.

4 **Listen.** Color and say. TR: 5

5 **Look.** Count and write.

6 **Listen.** Draw and color. TR: 6

7 Listen and say. TR: 7

8 Listen and look. Which word is different? Circle. TR: 8

1.

2.

9 Listen and chant. Point. TR: 9

Hello, hello.
Hi there, hi.

Time to go.
Bye, goodbye!

Unit 1

My School

1 Listen. Look and circle. TR: 10

1.

2.

3.

4.

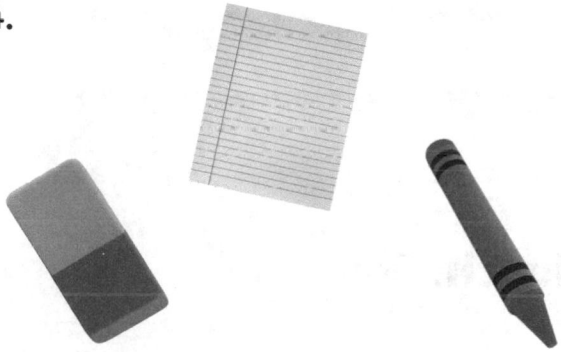

5.

6.

2 Listen and say. TR: 11

What is it?

It's a pen.

3 Cut out the cards on page 57. Listen. Glue the cards. Say. TR: 12

1	2	3	4
5	6	7	8

4 Match. Say.

5 **Listen.** Color and say. TR: 13

1. 
2. 
3. 
4. 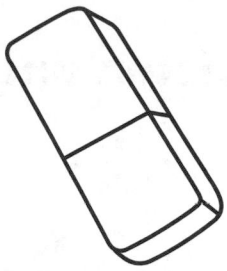

6 **Listen.** Color. Count and say. TR: 14

7 **Listen.** Count and write. TR: 15

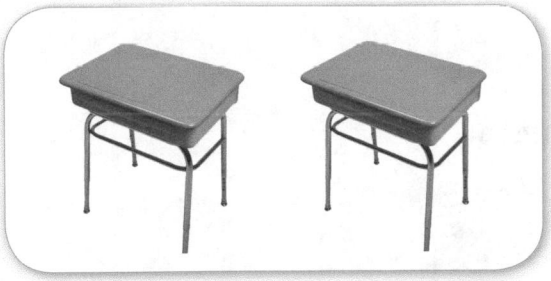

_____

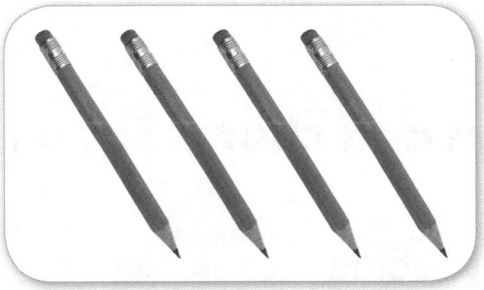

_____

_____

_____

8 Listen and say. TR: 16

9 Listen and look. Which word is different? Circle. TR: 17

1.

2.

3.

10 Listen and chant. Say a new verse. TR: 18

I have some 

I have a 

I have a 

Let's draw again!

I have an 

I have a 

I have some 

Let's draw again!

Unit 2

My Toys

1 **Listen.** Look and circle. TR: 19

1.

2.

3.

4.

5.

6.

2 Listen and say. TR: 20

3 Cut out the cards on page 57. Listen. What is it? Glue the cards. Say. TR: 21

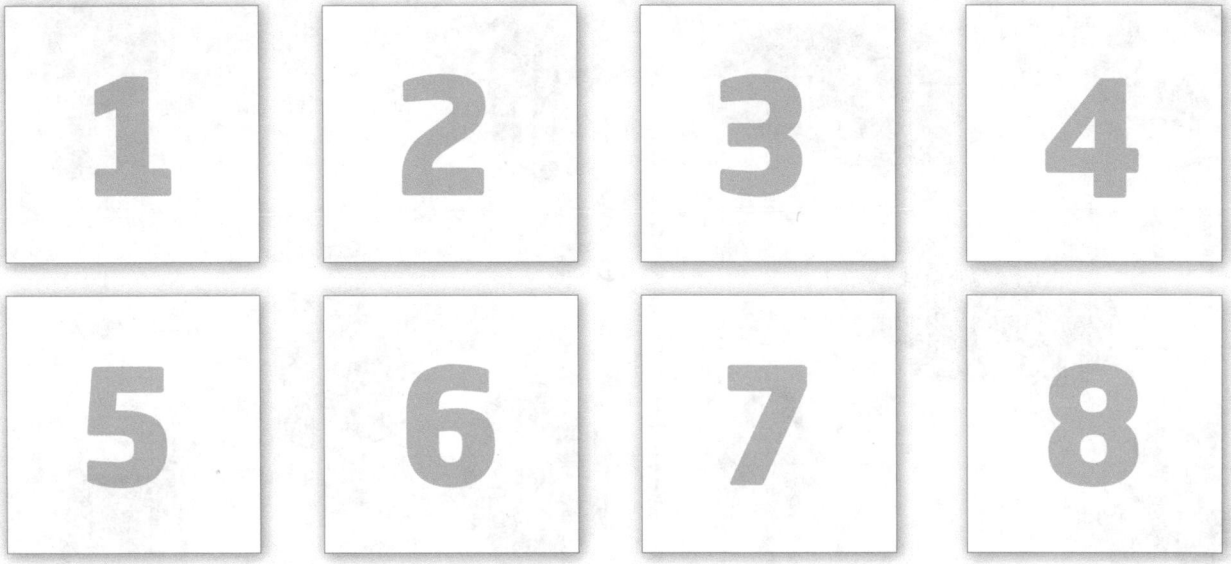

4 Draw your favorite toy. Color. What is it? Say.

5 **Listen.** Color and say. TR: 22

1.

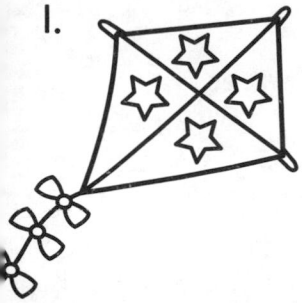

2.

3.

4.

6 **Listen.** Color. Count and say. TR: 23

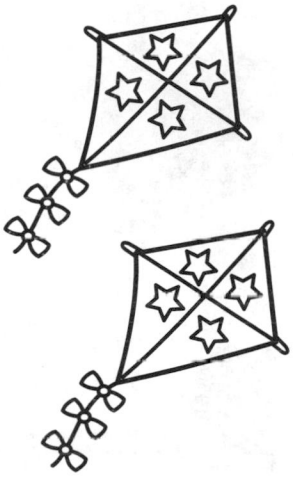

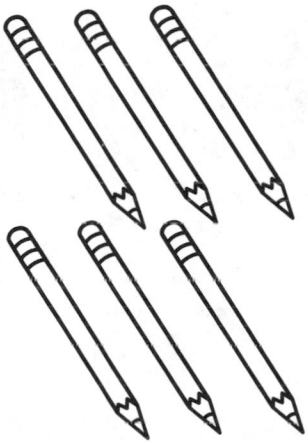

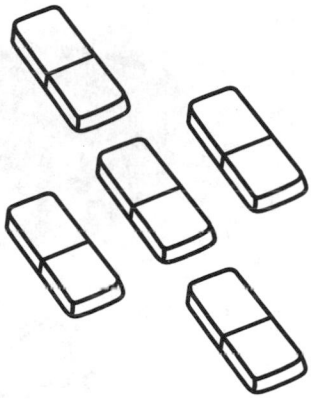

7 **Listen.** Count and write. TR: 24

_____

_____

_____

_____

8 Listen and say. TR: 25

9 Listen and look. Which word is different? Circle. TR: 26

1.

2.

3.

10 Listen and chant. Say a new verse. TR: 27

and

and more toys.

and

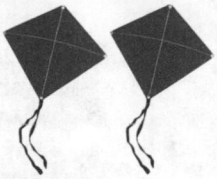

for girls and boys!

and

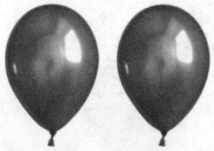

and more toys.

and

for girls and boys!

Unit 3

My Family

1 **Listen and look.** Draw a line. TR: 28

1
2
3
4
5
6
7
8
9
10

2 Listen and say. TR: 29

3 Listen and circle. TR: 30

1.  

2.  

3.  

4 Listen and say. TR: 31

5 Cut out the cards on page 59. Listen. Where's the family? Glue the cards. Say. TR: 32

6 **Listen.** Color and say. TR: 33

1.

2.

3.

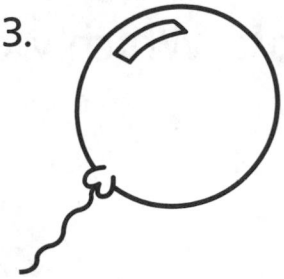

4.

7 **Listen.** Color. Count and say. TR: 34

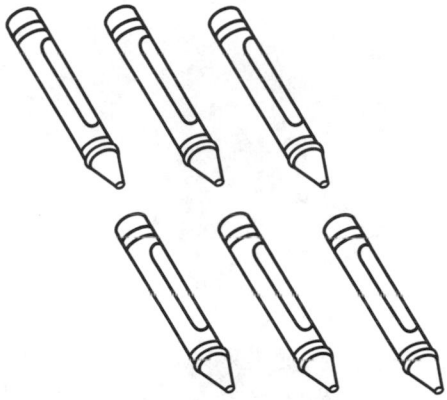

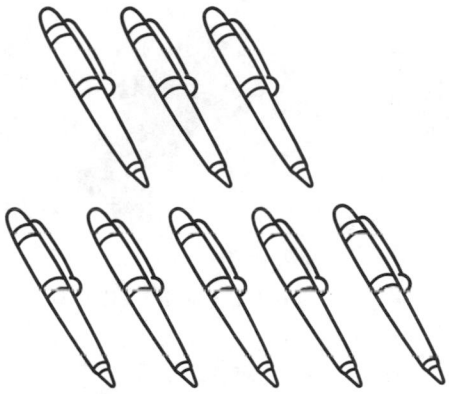

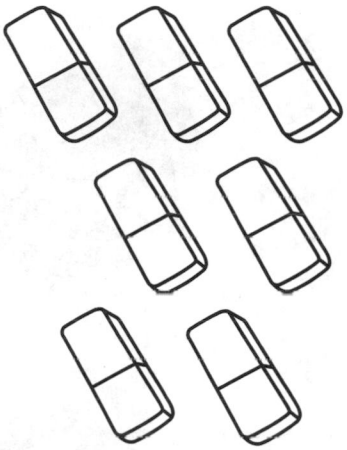

8 **Listen.** Count and write. TR: 35

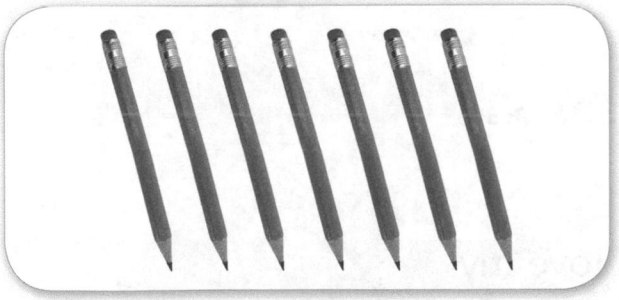

_____

_____

_____

_____

9 Listen and say. TR: 36

10 Listen and look. Which word is different? Circle. TR: 37

1.

2.

3.

11 Listen and chant. Say a new verse. TR: 38

I love my 

Oh yes, I do.

My  and my 

love him, too.

I love my 

Oh yes, I do.

My  and my 

love her, too.

Unit 4

My Body

1 **Listen and look.** Draw a line. TR: 39

2 Listen and say. TR: 40

I have 4 feet.

He has 4 feet.

3 Listen and circle. Say. TR: 41

1.

2.

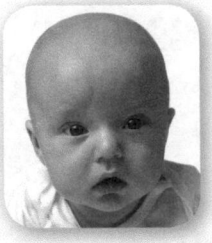

3.

4.

4 Cut out the cards on page 59. Listen and look. Glue the cards. Say. TR: 42

5 **Listen.** Color and say. TR: 43

1.

2.

3.

4.

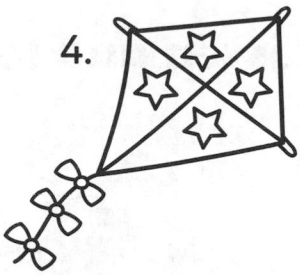

6 **Listen.** Color. Count and say. TR: 44

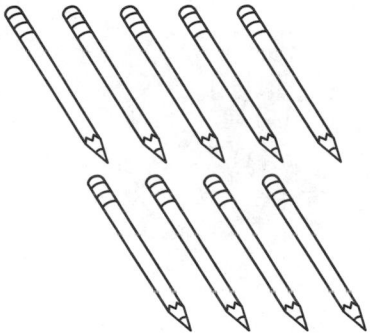

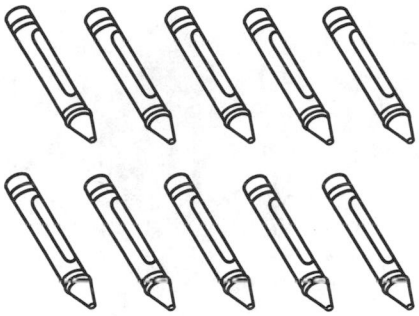

7 **Listen.** Count and write. TR: 45

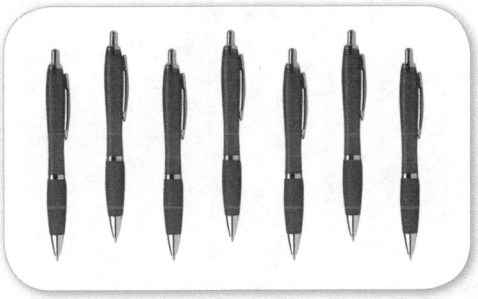

_____

_____

_____

_____

8 Listen and say. TR: 46

9 Listen and look. Which word is different? Circle. TR: 47

1.

2.

3.

10 Listen and chant. Say a new verse. TR: 48

One  for me.

Two  for you.

Two  for me.

Two 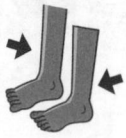 for you.

No  for me.

Brown  for you.

A  for me,

and  , too.
mustache

Units 1-4

Review

1 **Listen.** Look and circle. TR: 49

1.

2.

3.

4.

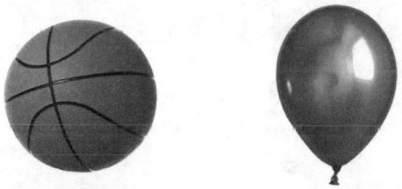

5.

6.

7.

8.

2 **Listen and color.** TR: 50

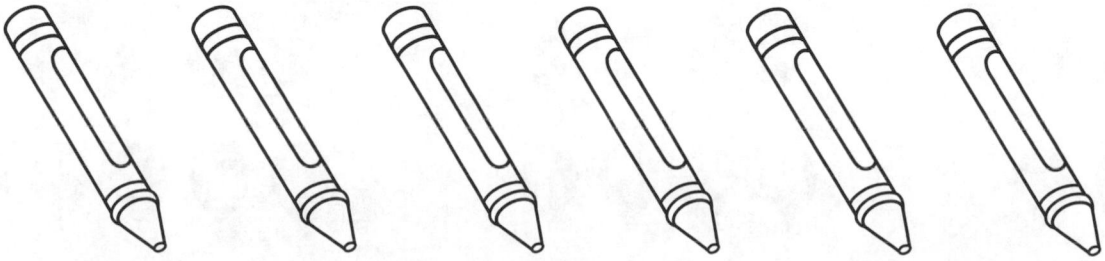

3 **Listen.** Look and circle. TR: 51

1.

2.

3.

4 **Listen.** Count and circle. TR: 52

1.

2.

3.

4.

Unit 5

Stories

1 **Listen.** Look and circle. TR: 53

1.

2.

3.

4.

5.

6.

2 **Listen.** Draw. TR: 54

1.

2.

3 **Listen and say.** TR: 55

4 **Cut out the cards on page 61.** Listen. Glue the cards. Say. TR: 56

1	2	3	4
5	6	7	8

5 **Draw.** What do you want? Say. Color.

6 **Listen.** Color and say. TR: 57

1.

2.

3.

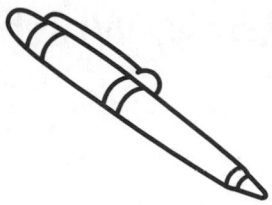

4.

7 **Listen.** Color. Count and say. TR: 58

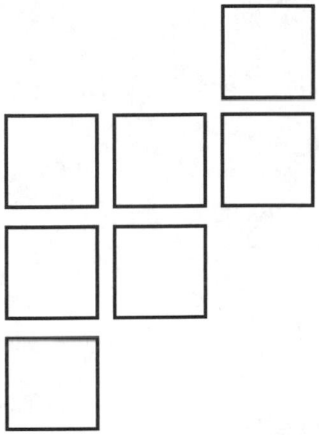

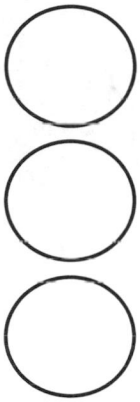

8 **Listen.** Count and write. TR: 59

_____

_____

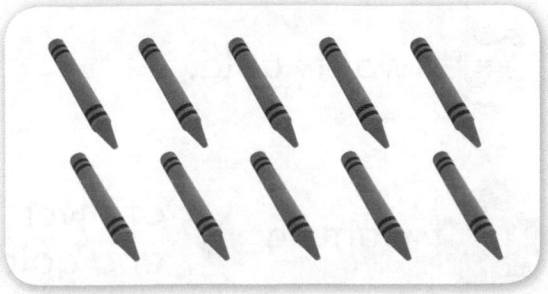

_____

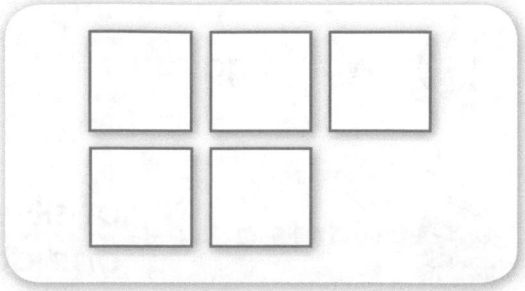

_____

9 Listen and say. TR: 60

10 Listen and look. Which word is different? Circle. TR: 61

1.

2.

3.

11 Listen and chant. Say a new verse. TR: 62

The  wants silver.

The  wants gold.

The  wants a  of silver *and* gold!

The  wants silver.

The  wants gold.

The  wants a  of silver *and* gold!

ring

Unit 6

I Like Food

1 **Listen.** Look and circle. TR: 63

1.

2.

3.

4.

5.

6.

2 Listen and say. TR: 64

3 Cut out the cards on page 61. Glue the cards. Say.

I like...

I don't like...

4 What is your favorite food? Draw.

5 **Listen and color.** Listen, count, and say. TR: 65

1.

2.

6 **Count and say.** How many circles? How many squares?

circles ____

squares ____

7 **Listen.** Count and say. TR: 66

____

____

____

____

____

8 Listen and say. TR: 67

9 Listen and look. Which word is different? Circle. TR: 68

1.

2.

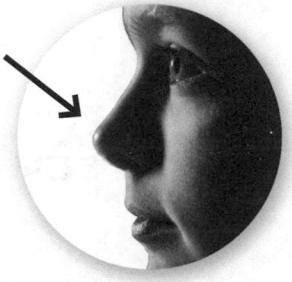

3.

10 Listen and chant. Say a new verse. TR: 69

I like 

I like 

I like 

They're so nice!

I like 

I like 

I like 

They're so nice!

Unit 7

Clothes

1 Listen and look. Draw a line. TR: 70

1
2
3
4
5
6
7
8

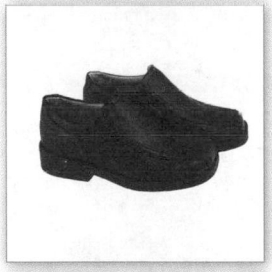

2 Listen and look. Draw a line. Color. TR: 71

Listen and say. TR: 72

It's hot. I'm wearing shorts.

It's cold. He's wearing a hat.

Cut out the cards on page 63. Listen. Glue the cards. Say. TR: 73

1	2	3	4
5	6	7	8

5 Connect the dots. What is it? Say. Color.

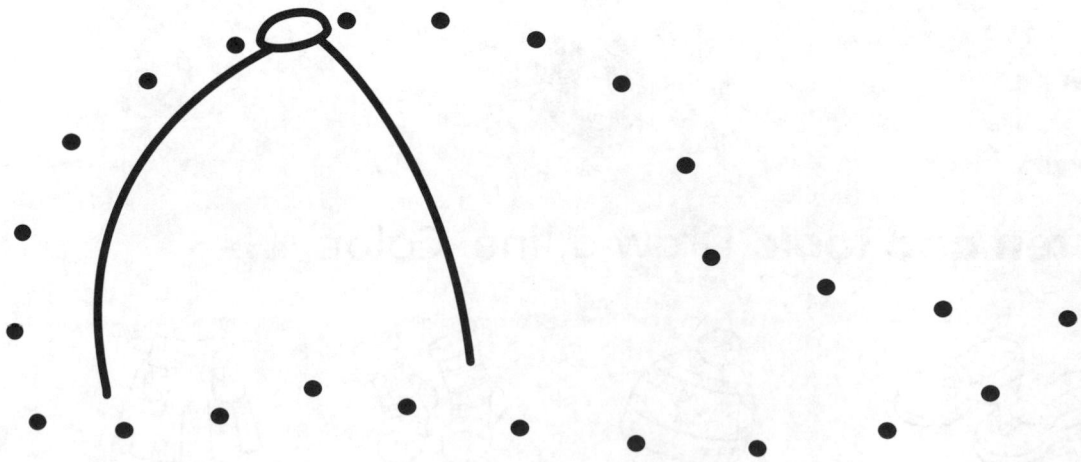

6 **Listen.** Color and say. TR: 74

1. 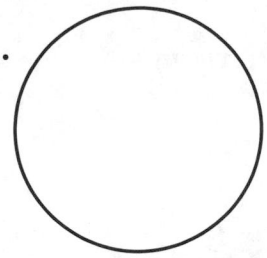
2. 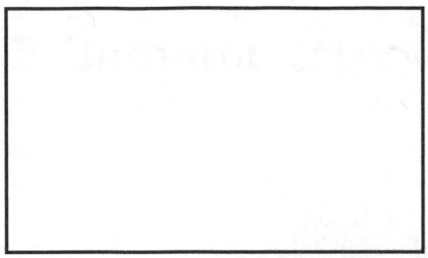
3. 
4. 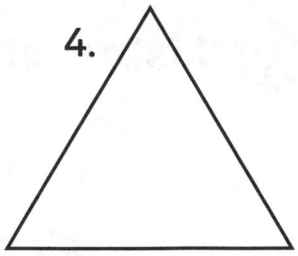

7 **Listen.** Color. Count and say. TR: 75

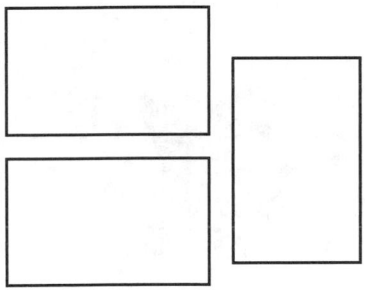

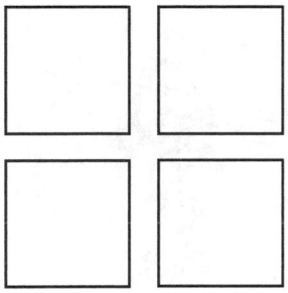

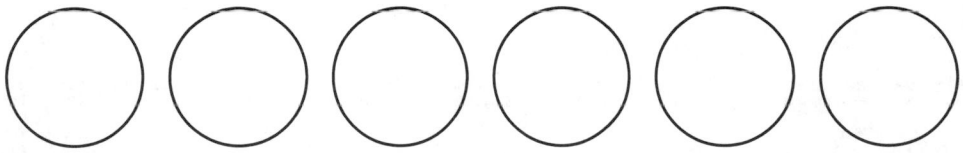

8 **Listen.** Count and write. TR: 76

_____

_____

_____

_____

9 Listen and say. TR: 77

10 Listen and look. Which word is different? Circle. TR: 78

1.

2.

3.

11 Listen and chant. Say a new verse. TR: 79

I want a 

My sister wants a 

Let's shop for clothes.

 please say yes!

I want some 

My sister wants a 

We want new clothes.

 please say yes!

Unit 8

Animals

1 Listen and look. Draw a line. TR: 80

1
2
3
4
5
6
7
8
9
10

2 Listen and say. TR: 81

3 Cut out the cards on page 63. Listen. Glue the cards. Say. TR: 82

1	2	3	4
5	6	7	8

4 Connect the dots. What is it? Say. Color.

5 **Listen.** Color and say. TR: 83

6 **Listen.** Color. Count and say. TR: 84

7 **Listen.** Count and write. TR: 85

_____

_____

_____

_____

8 Listen and say. TR: 86

9 Listen and look. Which word is different? Circle. TR: 87

1.

2.

3.

10 Listen and chant. Say a new verse. TR: 88

Look, I'm a
I walk and I run.

Look, I'm a
standing in the sun.

Look, I'm a
I walk and I run.

Look, I'm a
standing in the sun.

Units 5-8

Review

1 **Listen.** Look and circle. TR: 89

1.

2.

3.

4.

5.

6.

7.

8.

2 **Listen.** Look and circle. TR: 90

1.

2.

3.

3 **Listen and color.** TR: 91

4 **Listen.** Count and circle. TR: 92

1. 

2. 

3. 

4. 

5. 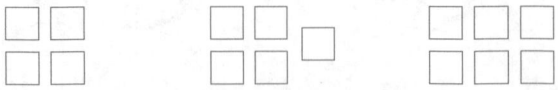

6. 

Trace and write.

Use with Unit I.

a a a

A A A

b b b

B B B

apple

paper

book

bye

Trace and write.

Use with Unit I.

c c c

C C C

1 1 1 2 2 2

3 3 3 4 4 4

crayon

pencil

chair

car

Trace and write.

Use with Unit 2.

d d d

D D D

e e e

E E E

pen

desk

teddy bear

Trace and write.

Use with Unit 2.

f

F

5

6

four

eraser

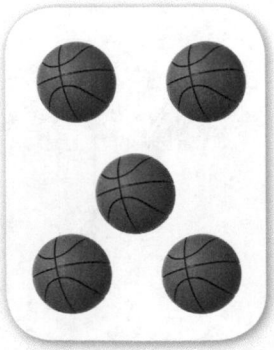

five

Trace and write.

Use with Unit 3.

g g g

G G G

h h h

H H H

father

mother

grandma

hello

Trace and write.

Use with Unit 3.

i

I

7

8

sisters

pencil

Mia

Eddie

Trace and write.

Use with Unit 4.

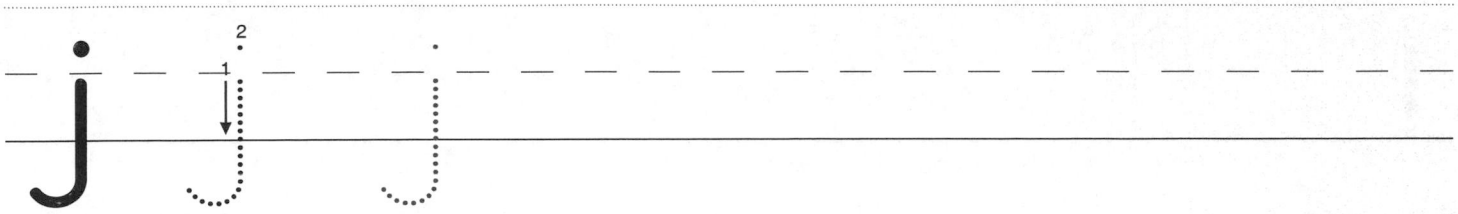

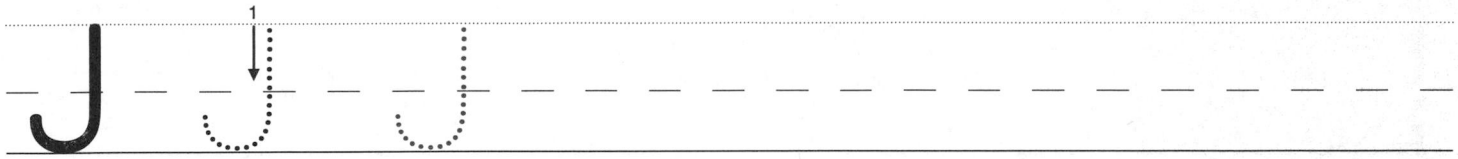

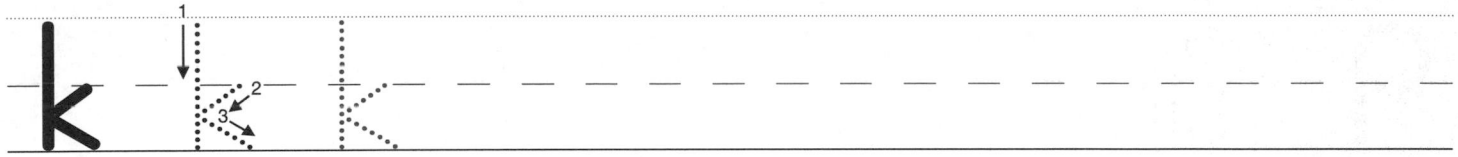

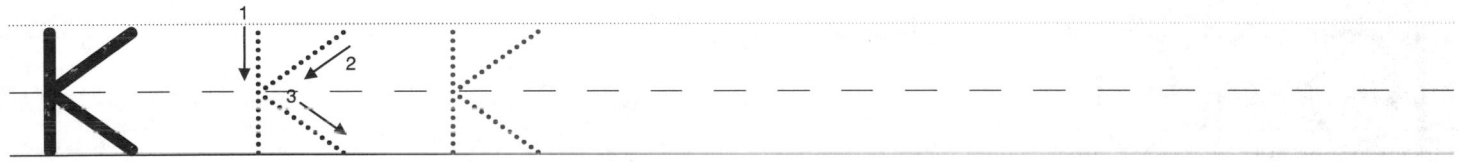

kite

kitchen

juice

truck

Trace and write.

Use with Unit 4.

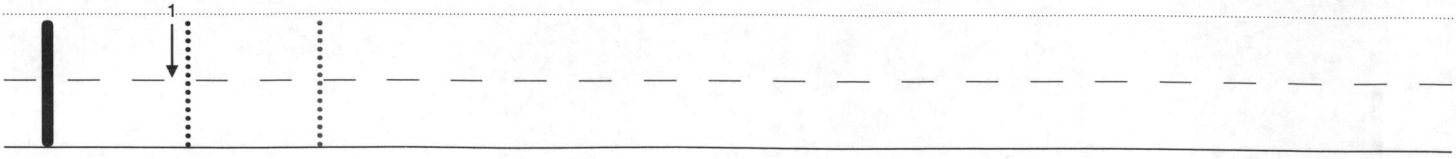

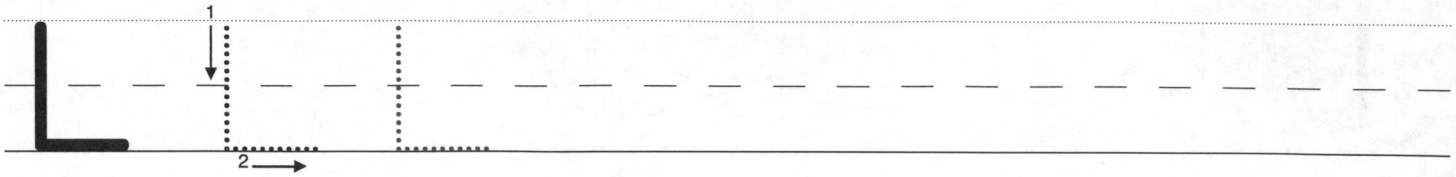

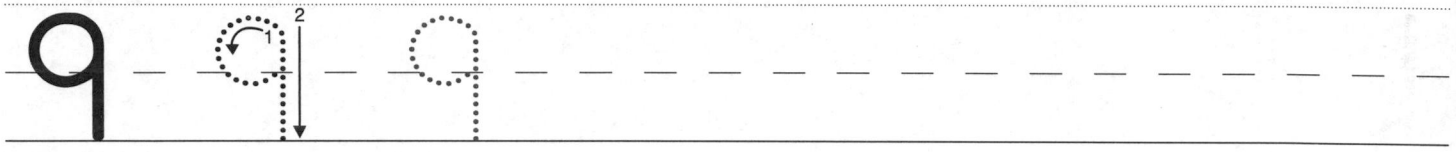

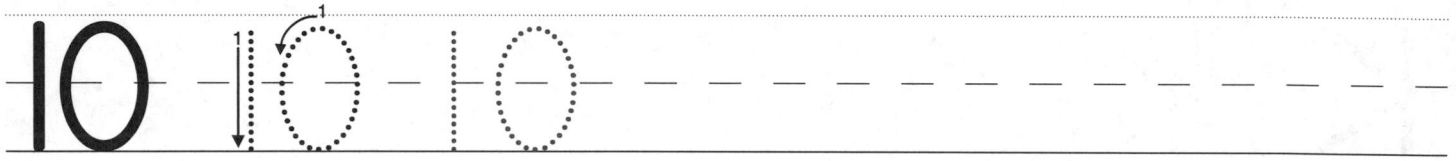

ball

balloon

doll

living room

Trace and write.

Use with Unit 5.

m m m

M M M

n n n

N N N

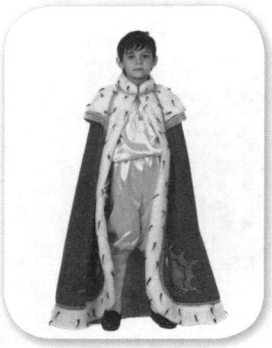

prince

grandma

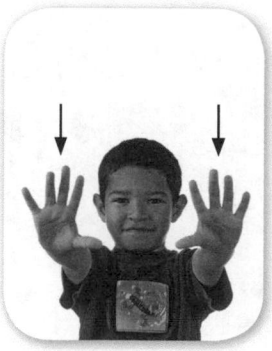

hands

friends

Trace and write.

Use with Unit 5.

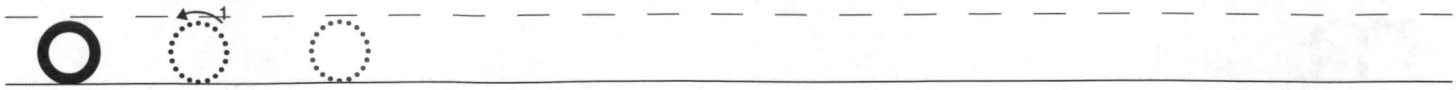

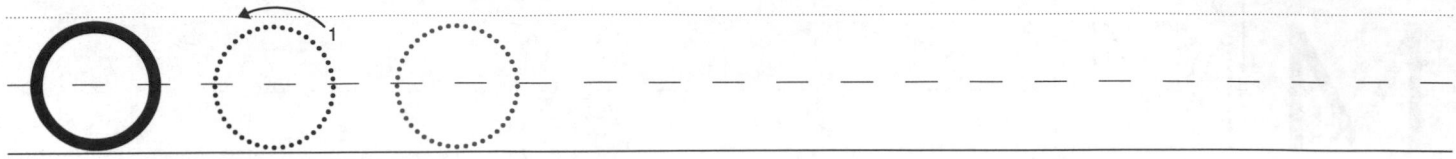

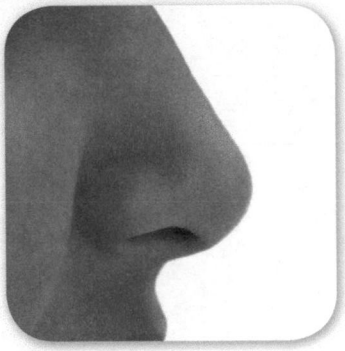

nose

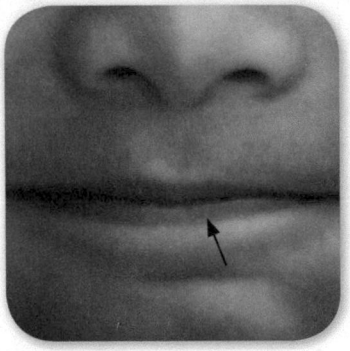

mouth

balloon

bathroom

robot

book

Trace and write.

Use with Unit 6.

p p p p

P P P P

q q q q

Q Q Q Q

pen

queen

pencil

paper

Trace and write.

Use with Unit 6.

r r r

R R R

grandpa

car

rice

prince

bread

crown

Trace and write.

Use with Unit 7.

s

S

t

T

socks

shorts

skirt

shirt

Trace and write.

Use with Unit 7.

u

U

v

V

Write your name.

Trace and write.

Use with Unit 8.

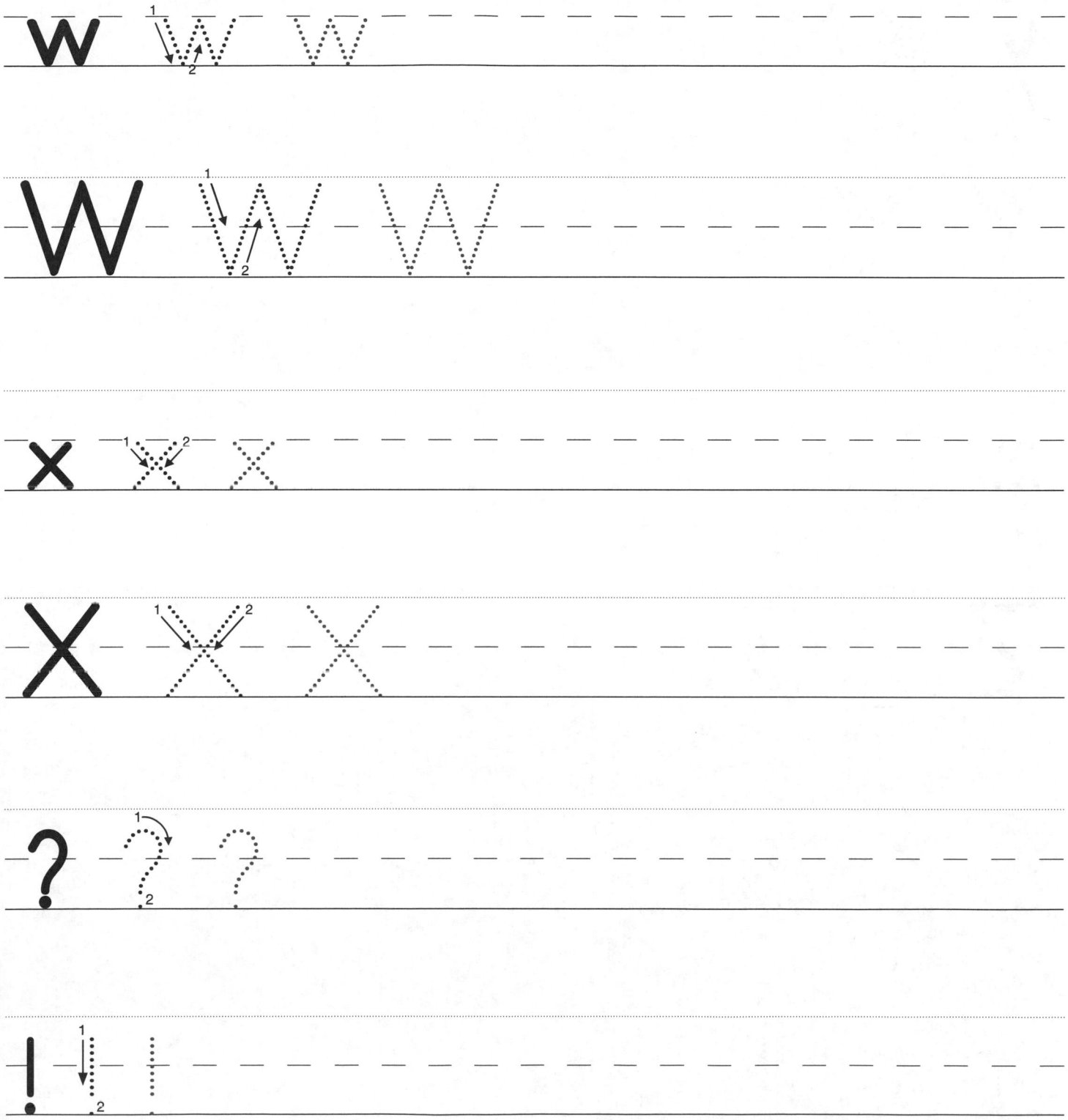

Trace and write.

Use with Unit 8.

y y y

Y Y Y

z z z

Z Z Z

Do you like school?

Yes, I do!

Unit 1 Use with Activity 3 on page 6.

Unit 2 Use with Activity 3 on page 10.

Unit 3 Use with Activity 5 on page 14.

Unit 4 Use with Activity 4 on page 18.

Unit 5 Use with Activity 4 on page 24.

Unit 6 Use with Activity 3 on page 28.

Unit 7 Use with Activity 4 on page 32.

Unit 8 Use with Activity 3 on page 36.